50 *Quick and Easy* PIZZAS

50 *Quick and Easy* PIZZAS

FAST, TASTY PIZZAS FOR EVERY OCCASION, SHOWN IN 300 PHOTOGRAPHS

SHIRLEY GILL

LORENZ BOOKS

This edition is published by Lorenz Books,
an imprint of Anness Publishing Ltd,
Blaby Road,
Wigston, Leicestershire
LE18 4SE; info@anness.com

www.lorenzbooks.com; www.annesspublishing.com

If you like the images in this book and would like to investigate using them
for publishing, promotions or advertising, please visit our website
www.practicalpictures.com for more information.

© Anness Publishing Ltd 2013

Publisher : Joanna Lorenz
Editors : Joanne Rippin, Anne Hildyard
Designer : Peter Laws
Photographer : Karl Adamson

For all recipes, quantities are given in both metric and imperial
measures and, where appropriate, measures are also given in standard
cups and spoons. Follow one set, but not a mixture because they are not
interchangeable.

PUBLISHER'S NOTE
Although the advice and information in this book are believed to be accurate
and true at the time of going to press, neither the authors nor the publisher
can accept any legal responsibility or liability for any errors or omissions
that may have been made nor for any inaccuracies nor for any loss, harm or
injury that comes about from following instructions or advice in this book.

Contents

Introduction

The pizza originated as a cheap, savoury snack in Naples, sold from street stalls or in special eating houses, but it is now a universally popular main meal. Today's favourite fast food, pizzas are quick and filling meals for people in a hurry. However, if you take the time to make your own you will find they are easy and fun - the simplest are often the best, provided the ingredients are fresh and flavoursome. There is a topping to suit everyone, and they can be as generous and varied as you wish.

Below: Mini Focaccia with Pine Nuts make a tasty lunch or supper. Just serve with a tomato salad for a light meal.

In this book you will find instructions on how to make basic pizza dough as well as several delicious variations. The amount of dough needed for one recipe is small and very easy to handle, and preparations are simple and easy. If using ready-made bases, these recipes can be made in under an hour.

A word on baking pizzas: the very best results are achieved by cooking them in a traditional brick oven to make them light and crisp. Even without a brick oven, the home cook can achieve excellent results with a pizza brick, which helps distribute the heat evenly, and extracts moisture. The direct heat makes them wonderfully crisp. A simple unglazed terracotta tile works well. Pizzas must be eaten hot straight from the oven since they soon harden.

Pizzas need not be served just as snacks or main meals; they can become stylish starters, when they are made as small pizzettes or served in thin wedges. They also make great party food – a festive array of pizzas will please any crowd!

This is a collection for pizza lovers everywhere. Although most of the recipes contain cheese, this can be reduced if you want a lighter pizza. There is also a final section of interesting Italian breads, full of great flavours and textures just waiting to be tasted.

Right: Here are all the delicious ingredients for a great pizza: Parmesan cheese, basil, tomatoes, garlic and pizza dough.

Herbs and Spices

Herbs and spices are essential for seasoning pizzas. Fresh herbs should be used if possible. Buy growing herbs in pots: this ensures the herbs are fresh, and provides a continuous supply.

Basil (sweet basil)
Intensely aromatic, basil has a distinctive peppery flavour. The leaves can be used to garnish pizzas and are also a perfect partner for tomatoes in a summer salad; chopped or shredded basil can become the main seasoning ingredient.

Black peppercorns
Best used freshly ground in a mill or crushed since the taste and aroma of peppercorns disappears quickly.

Chillies (fresh and dried chilli products)
Fresh chillies vary in taste, from mild to fiery hot. Generally the large, round fleshy varieties are milder than the small, thin-skinned pointed ones. For a milder, spicy flavour, remove the seeds and veins.

Red chilli flakes are made from dried, crushed chillies and are somewhat milder than fresh chillies. They can be heated with olive oil to make chilli oil for brushing over pizza bases or used to add bite to pizza toppings and fillings for calzone.

Mild chilli powder is a commercially prepared mixture of chilli, ground herbs and spices. It can be used to flavour more contemporary-styled pizzas.

Chives
A member of the onion family, the long, narrow green leaves are good used as a garnish, added to salads, or snipped and mixed into the pizza dough to add extra flavour.

Coriander (Cilantro)
The delicate light green leaves have an unusual flavour and distinctive aroma. Chopped leaves are often used in combination with chillies, and especially in Californian-style pizzas. The fresh leaves also make an attractive garnish.

Cumin
These seeds have a warm, earthy flavour and aromatic fragrance and are sold whole or ground. Use in pizzas, especially those with chilli and oregano, for a Mexican flavour.

Curly parsley
This provides colour and gives a fresh flavour to pizza toppings.

Flat-leaf parsley (Italian parsley)
This variety has a slightly different flavour from common curly parsley, but they can be used interchangeably.

Herbes de Provence
A dried herb mixture of thyme, savory, rosemary, marjoram and oregano. It is particularly good mixed with black olives, added to pizza doughs or sprinkled on top before cooking.

Nutmeg
With a sweetish, highly aromatic flavour, nutmeg has an affinity for rich foods. It is used to great effect in stuffed pizzas and pizza toppings, especially those containing spinach.

Oregano
An aromatic and highly flavoured herb. Oregano features strongly in Italian cooking, in which it is sprinkled on pizzas.

Rosemary
With its pungent, pine-like aroma, rosemary can be overpowering, but when used judiciously, it can add a delicious flavour to vegetables such as potatoes for an unusual pizza topping.

Saffron
The dried stigmas of the saffron crocus, saffron is the most expensive spice in the world, but very little is needed in most recipes, sometimes as little as a pinch. Pungent with a brilliant yellow colour, saffron is available as strands or ground.

Sage
Just a few leaves can deliciously flavour a pizza topping, especially with a rich-tasting cheese like Gorgonzola; sage tends to overpower subtle flavours.

Salt
Because it balances the action of yeast, salt is an integral part of bread-making. For seasoning, use sea salt flakes or refined table salt; the former has a slightly stronger flavour so use it sparingly.

Thyme
This is good chopped or crumbled, and stirred into tomato sauce or sprinkled on to pizzas. Sprigs can be used as a garnish.

Chives

Coriander (cilantro)

Saffron

Red chilli flakes

Mild chilli powder

Fresh red chillies

Nutmeg

Thyme

Curly parsley

Flat-leaf parsley
(Italian parsley)

Ground cumin

Herbes de Provence

Sea salt

Sage

Rosemary

Oregano

Basil

Black peppercorns

Fresh Vegetables for Pizzas

When making vegetable pizzas, use a mixture of vegetables that will look appealing together. Top with some sliced Mozzarella cheese or grated Parmesan for additional flavour.

Never has vegetable cookery been so exciting. A quick glance in the greengrocers and super-markets reveals a vast choice. There are baby aubergines (eggplant), wild mushrooms, red onions, colourful peppers (bell peppers), hot-tasting chillies, as well as fennel and wonderful asparagus – a truly international offering, providing endless possibilities to the cook.

As vegetables are so full of colour they make attractive and tempting pizza toppings, and making your own can cost less, as well as being healthier.

Choose the best quality fresh vegetables for maximum flavour and beautiful colour combinations. Think yellow (bell) pepper, red onion and spinach for a vibrant-looking pizza, and try to use vegetables that are newly in season.

Some should be pre-cooked – mushrooms, courgettes (zucchini) and aubergines (eggplant) for example – and some are used raw – onions, leek and tomato slices. Always drain cooked vegetables well and pat dry using kitchen paper, before topping your pizza dough. And of course, sun-dried tomatoes, olives and capers add a delightful piquancy, which will liven up any vegetable pizza.

Roasted vegetables also make a good topping for pizzas, try courgettes (zucchini), onions, (bell) peppers and tomatoes with fresh herbs such as basil and parsley sprinkled on top.

A southeast Asian flavour can be achieved by stir-frying pak choi, bean sprouts, broccoli florets, onions and sugar snap peas or mangetout. Add a sprinkling of soy sauce, sesame oil and mirin then spread over the pizza base.

Ring the changes by using fresh herbs, such as rosemary, chives, dill and coriander (cilantro). Vegetable pizzas are not just for vegetarians; they are for anyone who enjoys exciting food, inventively prepared and presented with style.

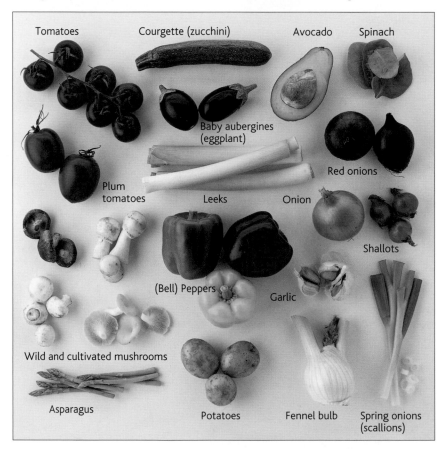

Tomatoes

Courgette (zucchini)

Avocado

Spinach

Baby aubergines (eggplant)

Plum tomatoes

Leeks

Onion

Red onions

Shallots

(Bell) Peppers

Garlic

Wild and cultivated mushrooms

Asparagus

Potatoes

Fennel bulb

Spring onions (scallions)

Meat and Fish for Pizzas

Pizzas are endlessly versatile, and can be made with many combinations of ingredients. If they are topped with meat or fish and some vegetables, you have a complete and satisfying meal.

Pizzas with a meat or fish topping make a substantial lunch or supper dish when served with a tossed salad, carrot and celery sticks or a vegetable platter. They can be topped with a wealth of delicious ingredients. Sliced cured meats, salamis, ham and spicy sausages are all popular topping ingredients. Chicken and minced (ground) beef can also be used in imaginative ways.

Fresh fish and shellfish also make tempting pizza toppings. Favourites such as prawns (shrimp), mussels, squid and salmon may be used alone or mixed for a good variety of flavours. Canned fish such as tuna and anchovies are ideal to make quick pizza toppings. If you find anchovies too salty, it helps to soak them in milk before use. For best results, add fresh fish and shellfish halfway through the cooking time to ensure that they do not overcook.

Pancetta

Sausages

Chorizo

Parma ham

Dressed crab

Smoked chicken

Prawns (shrimp)

Italian salami

Smoked ham

Minced (ground) beef

Pepperoni

Chicken

Smoked salmon

Mixed seafood

Storecupboard

If you keep the following ingredients to hand, you can easily rustle up a pizza with your standby storecupboard items. Just add fresh herbs and vegetables if you have them.

Anchovies
Canned anchovies have been filleted and salted then packed in oil. They are an important flavouring ingredient and garnish for many pizzas.

Artichoke hearts
Those packed in oil in jars are ideal for pizza toppings.

Capers
These are the flower buds of a Mediterranean shrub. They are preserved in vinegar and salt or salt alone. They have a strong piquant flavour.

Cornmeal (polenta flour)
Adds texture and an earthy flavour to the basic pizza dough.

Easy-blend dried yeast
Much faster and quicker to use than fresh or dried yeast, it does not need to be reconstituted in liquid first; but is mixed directly with the flour. Use lukewarm liquid as extreme temperatures can kill the yeast and the dough will not rise.

Olives
Green olives are unripe; black are ripe and have more flavour. They are available whole or pitted, or stuffed with ingredients such as pimientoes or anchovy fillets. You can buy them preserved in brine or oil. Pitted olives can be baked into bread or simply used as a garnish on pizzas.

Flour
White flour contains 72–74 per cent of the wheat grain. It is available in strong, plain (all-purpose) and self-raising (self-rising) forms. Traditional pizza bases are made from bread dough, which is usually made with strong white (stone-ground) flour with a high gluten content. Some strong white flours are bleached; "unbleached" is untreated flour. Plain white flour is used to make a flat bread called focaccia. Self-raising white flour has leavening or raising agents added to it, and is suitable for a scone pizza base. Wholemeal (whole-wheat) flour is milled from the whole grain. Strong and self-raising wholemeal flours are used for making pizza doughs. Mix it with white flour to get a lighter dough.

Olive oil
A good quality olive oil is brushed on the dough and a drizzle over the topping offers flavour and also protection in the fierce heat of the oven. Extra virgin olive oil is a darker green with a more intense flavour.

Pimientos
The Spanish word for pepper, pimientos are packed whole in cans, and are sweet, with a bright red colour.

Pine nuts
These small, oval, creamy coloured nuts with a sweet flavour can be sprinkled on to pizzas, or used in sauces such as pesto.

Red pesto
A richly aromatic sauce of pesto and sun-dried tomatoes. Delicious spread on pizza bases or added to tomato sauce.

Sun-dried tomato paste
This has a rich, intense flavour and makes a quick pizza topping. It also enriches sauces and gives a lovely colour.

Tapenade
This paste is made from ground green or black olives with olive oil. Delicious on pizza bases, especially those with goat's cheese.

Tomatoes: canned
Canned tomatoes come whole or chopped, for use in sauces and toppings.

Tomatoes: sun-dried in oil
Sun-dried tomatoes have a concentrated, salty flavour, which is tasty used in breads and as a pizza topping. If bought loose they are soaked in warm water before use.

Tomato purée (paste)
Useful for adding colour, intensity and flavour to homemade tomato sauce.

Tuna
Canned tuna fish is usually packed in oil, brine or water. Its firm texture makes it a useful pizza topping.

Walnuts
Nuts, especially walnuts are excellent added to bread to serve with antipasti.

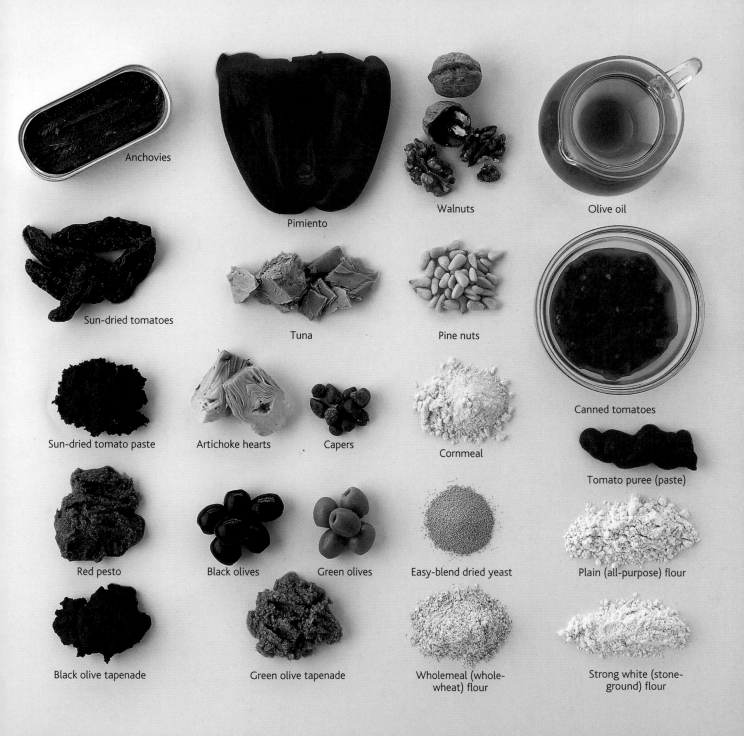

Anchovies

Pimiento

Walnuts

Olive oil

Sun-dried tomatoes

Tuna

Pine nuts

Canned tomatoes

Sun-dried tomato paste

Artichoke hearts

Capers

Cornmeal

Tomato puree (paste)

Red pesto

Black olives

Green olives

Easy-blend dried yeast

Plain (all-purpose) flour

Black olive tapenade

Green olive tapenade

Wholemeal (whole-wheat) flour

Strong white (stone-ground) flour

Pizza Cheeses

One of the most important elements in a tasty pizza is the cheese. Mozzarella is most often associated with pizza, but many cheeses can be used, so try different ones to suit your taste.

Bavarian smoked cheese
This has a pale creamy colour and mild, smoky flavour and a smooth, soft texture.

Cheddar
Flavours vary from mild to strong. It is an ideal cheese for cooking.

Dolcelatte
An Italian blue-veined, semi-soft cheese with a smooth, creamy texture and delicate piquant flavour.

Edam
A Dutch ball-shaped cheese, firm and smooth in texture with a mild flavour.

Feta
A crumbly cheese with a salty flavour, feta should be rinsed before using.

Goat's cheese
Generally shaped in logs, rounds, pyramids or ovals, it ranges from fresh and creamy to strong and tangy.

Gorgonzola piccante
This cheese is pleasantly sharp in flavour, with a softish paste and blue-green veins.

Gruyère
A hard cheese with a sweet and nutty taste, it is a good melting cheese.

Mozzarella
This versatile cheese is used in many pizza recipes for its melting quality. It should be white, fairly elastic and moist when cut.

Oak-smoked Cheddar
A Cheddar variant which adds a distinctive flavour when grated on pizzas.

Parmesan
This is grated for cooking and topping pizza. Freshly grated Parmesan is the best.

Pecorino
An Italian sheep's cheese which has a fairly strong distinctive flavour.

Red Leicester
This cheese has a mild flavour and a bright orange colour.

Ricotta
A soft Italian whey cheese with a delicate, smooth flavour. It is ideal for use in fillings for calzone and panzerotti.

Smoked mozzarella
This cheese has a smoky taste, and it has excellent melting properties.

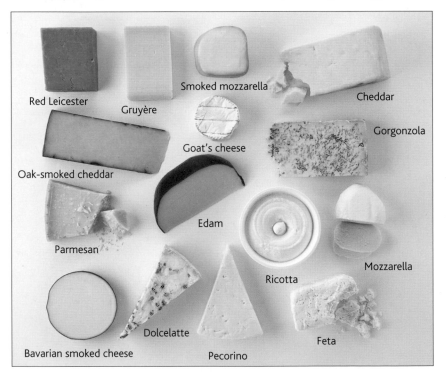

Red Leicester • Gruyère • Smoked mozzarella • Cheddar • Goat's cheese • Gorgonzola • Oak-smoked cheddar • Edam • Mozzarella • Parmesan • Ricotta • Dolcelatte • Feta • Bavarian smoked cheese • Pecorino

Equipment

To make pizzas successfully you do not have to have specialist tools, but many tasks are made simpler with the aid of certain utensils and gadgets.

Baking sheet
Choose a large heavy baking sheet that will not warp at high temperatures.

Box grater
A multi-surfaced grater with a fine and coarse sides can be used for all grating purposes.

Cook's knife
This has a heavy, wide blade that is ideal for chopping.

Flour dredger
A useful piece of equipment for dusting the work surface.

Garlic press
A small gadget used for crushing garlic.

Measuring jug
For measuring liquid, they are available in a wide range of sizes.

Mixing bowls
Bowls in various sizes are essential.

Nutmeg grater
A small grater for grating whole nutmegs.

Rolling pin
Choose a long, heavy pin for even rolling.

Spoons
To measure small amounts of ingredients. Metal spoons are oval with a pointed end. Wooden spoons are an essential item.

Swiss-roll tin
A rectangular tin, ideal for making pizzas.

Oil can
Usually made of metal it has a long, small spout for drizzling oil on to pizzas.

Olive stoner
This removes stones with one quick press.

Paring knife
A small knife for trimming and peeling vegetables.

Parmesan grater
A special grater for Parmesan.

Pastry brush/cutter
For brushing on oil, water or beaten egg white, and cutter to stamp out dough.

Pizza brick (Pizza stone)
A terracotta round, used as a baking sheet or pizza pan.

Pizza cutter/lifter/wheel
A dual-purpose gadget for cutting and serving pizzas. A wheel is used for slicing.

Pizza pan
Can be round and shallow or a deep pan. A perforated pan allows steam to escape and encourages a crisp base.

Basic Pizza Dough

This simple bread base is rolled out thinly on a lightly floured surface for a traditional pizza recipe. It makes an authentically Italian, thin crispy base, which is perfect with most toppings.

Makes
1 x 25–30cm/10–12in round pizza base
4 x 13cm/5in round pizza bases
1 x 30 x 18cm 12 x 7in oblong pizza base

175g/6oz/1½ cups strong white flour
1.25ml/¼tsp salt
5ml/1 tsp easy-blend dried yeast
120–150ml/4–5 fl oz/½–⅔ cup
　　lukewarm water
15ml/1 tbsp olive oil

1 Sift the flour and salt into a large mixing bowl.

2 Using a wooden spoon, stir in the dried yeast.

3 Make a well in the centre of the dry ingredients. Pour in the water and oil and mix with a spoon to a soft dough.

4 Knead the dough or a lightly floured surface for about 10 minutes until smooth and elastic.

COOK'S TIP
If you make your dough in advance, always cover with clear film and leave in the refrigerator until you are ready to use it. You can freeze the pizza dough once it has been knocked back in step 6. Either wrap all the dough and freeze it, or if you are making 4 small pizzas, divide the dough into 4, wrap each and freeze.

5 Place the dough in a greased bowl and cover with clear film. Leave in a warm place to rise (for about 1 hour or until the dough has doubled in size).

6 Knock back the dough (remove excess air by kneading the dough roughly). Turn on to a lightly floured surface and knead again for 2–3 minutes. Roll out the dough as required and place on a greased baking sheet. Work around the edge, pushing up the dough with your fingers to make a rim. The dough is now ready for topping.

Deep-pan Pizza Dough

Traditionally preferred by hungry diners instead of the lighter, thinner pizza, this recipe produces a deep and spongy base.

Makes
1 x 25cm/10in deep-pan pizza base

225g/8oz/2 cups strong white (stone-ground) flour
2.5ml/½ tsp salt
5ml/1 tsp easy-blend dried yeast
150ml/¼ pint/⅔ cup lukewarm water
30ml/2 tbsp olive oil

Follow the method for Basic Pizza Dough. When the dough has doubled in size, knock back and knead for 2–3 minutes. Roll out the dough to fit a greased 25cm/10in deep-pan pizza tin or sandwich tin. Prove for 10 minutes, roll out to desired size, then add the topping.

Wholemeal Pizza Dough

75g/3oz/1½ cups strong wholemeal (whole-wheat) flour
75g/3oz/1½ cups strong white (stone-ground) flour
1.25ml/¼ tsp salt
5ml/1 tsp easy-blend dried yeast
120–150ml/4–5fl oz/½–⅔ cup lukewarm water
15ml/1 tbsp olive oil

Follow the method for Basic Pizza Dough. You may have to add a little extra water to form a soft dough, depending on the absorbency of the flour.

COOK'S TIP
Pep up your dough by sprinkling in a little of your favourite spices or seeds such as sesame or fennel. Top with leaves of chopped fresh herbs – try basil or oregano on cheese and tomato pizzas; tarragon for chicken pizzas; dill with salmon or seafood pizzas; and parsley and chives for vegetable pizzas.

Cornmeal Pizza Dough

175g/6oz/1½ cups strong white (stone-ground) flour
25g/1oz/½ cup cornmeal
1.25ml/¼ tsp salt
5ml/1 tsp easy-blend dried yeast
120— 150 ml/4–5 fl oz/½–⅔ cup lukewarm water
15ml/1 tbsp olive oil

Follow the method for Basic Pizza Dough. Cornmeal makes a strong crust, allowing for generous toppings. The cornmeal base has a distinctive taste and texture and is high in fibre, making it more filling.

Ready-made Bases

Fortunately for the busy cook it is now possible to buy fresh, frozen or long-life pizza bases from most supermarkets. Many are enriched with additional ingredients like cheese, herbs and onions. Although they never seem to taste as good as a real home-made pizza base they can be very useful to keep on hand. All you have to do is add your chosen topping and bake in the usual way. Ready-made bases can be livened up by spreading with tapenade or pesto and a sprinkling of chopped fresh herbs, then a tasty topping.

Scone Pizza Dough

A scone mixture is so quick to make and uses storecupboard ingredients, so you can easily whip up a pizza. The mixture uses butter instead of oil, milk rather than water, and raising (rising) flour instead of strong white (stone-ground) flour.

Makes
1 x 25cm/10in round pizza base
1 x 30 x 18cm/12 x 7in oblong pizza base

115g/4oz/1 cup self-raising
   (self-rising) flour
115g/4oz/1 cup self-raising (self-rising)
   wholemeal flour
pinch of salt
50g/2oz/4 tbsp butter, diced
about 150ml/¼ pint/⅔ cup milk

1 Mix together the flours and salt in a mixing bowl. Rub in the butter until the mixture resembles fine breadcrumbs.

2 Add the milk and mix with a wooden spoon to a soft dough.

3 Knead lightly on a lightly floured surface until smooth. The dough is now ready to roll out.

Superquick Pizza Dough

If you're really pressed for time, try a packet pizza dough mix. For best results roll out the dough to a 25–30cm/10–12in circle; this is slightly larger than stated on the packet, but it does produce a perfect thin, crispy base. For a deep-pan version use two packets.

Makes
4 x 13 cm/5in round pizza bases
1 x 30 x 18cm/12 x 7in oblong pizza base

I x 150g/5oz packet pizza base mix
120ml/4fl oz/½ cup lukewarm water

1 Empty the contents of the packet into a mixing bowl.

2 Pour in the water and mix with a wooden spoon to a soft dough.

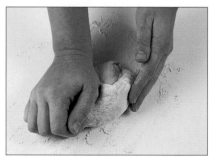

3 Turn the dough on to a lightly floured surface and knead for 5 minutes until smooth and elastic. The dough is now ready to use.

Using a Food Processor

For speed, make the pizza dough in a food processor; let the machine do the mixing and kneading, then leave the dough in a warm place for 1 hour to prove until it has doubled in size.

1 Put the flour, salt and yeast into a food processor. Process to mix.

2 Measure the water into a jug and add the oil. With the machine running, add the liquid and process until the dough forms a soft ball Leave to rest for 2 minutes, then process for 1 minute more to knead the dough.

3 Remove the dough from the processor and shape into a neat round. Place in a greased bowl and cover with clear film. Leave in a warm place for about 1 hour until doubled in size. Knock back and knead the dough for 2–3 minutes. The dough is now ready to use.

Using a Bread Machine

Almost any pizza dough can be adapted for the bread machine, which will do all the work for you, such as the mixing, kneading and rising, leaving you free to prepare other food.

Makes
1 x 25–30cm/10–12in round pizza base
4 x 13cm/5in round pizza bases
1 x 30 x 18cm 12 x 7in oblong pizza base

175g/6oz/1½ cups strong white flour
1.25ml/¼tsp salt
5ml/1 tsp easy-blend dried yeast
120–150ml/4–5 fl oz/½–⅔ cup
    lukewarm water
15ml/1 tbsp olive oil

1 Put the flour, salt and yeast into the pan of the bread machine. Add the water and olive oil.

2 Place the pan in the machine and select the dough cycle or pizza dough setting. Press the start button and leave it until the cycle is complete. Spray or grease a pizza pan and either press the dough into the pan or roll it out. Add your chosen topping and bake the pizza.

COOK'S TIP
The dough can be frozen; just wrap it in clear film and freeze. When you want to use it, defrost in the refrigerator or for a few hours in the kitchen. Shape and stretch or roll it out to use.

Stoning (Pitting) Olives

Using a stoner (pitter) is the easiest way to remove the stone from an olive, but you can also use a small sharp knife. The stones from olives with a softer flesh can easily be taken out by hand.

1 Put the olive in the stoner (pitter) with the pointed end uppermost.

2 Squeeze the handles together to extract the stone, and discard.

Chopping Herbs

Either use a heavy chef's knife or a special piece of equipment called a mezzaluna, which has a two-handled curved blade that is rocked back and forward until the herbs are chopped as coarse or fine as you require.

1 Strip the leaves from the stalk and pile them on a chopping board.

COOK'S TIP
Before chopping herbs, wash the leaves, removing any wilted or damaged ones, then discard any coarse stalks.

2 Using a sharp knife cut the herbs into small pieces, holding the tip of the blade against the board and rocking the blade back and forth. Move the herbs around and keep chopping until they are as fine as you want them to be.

Tomato Sauce

Tomato sauce forms the basis of the topping in many of the recipes. Make sure it is well seasoned and thick before spreading it over the base. It will keep fresh in a covered container in the fridge for up to 3 days.

One quantity covers
2 x 25–30cm/10–12in round pizza base
4 x 30 x 18cm/12 x 7in oblong pizza base

**Makes around 450ml/³⁄₄ pint/
    scant 2 cups**
15ml/1 tbsp olive oil
1 onion, finely chopped
1 garlic clove, crushed
1 x 400g/14oz can chopped tomatoes
15ml/l tbsp tomato purée
15ml/1 tbsp chopped fresh mixed
    herbs, such as parsley, thyme, basil
    and oregano
pinch of sugar
salt and black pepper

1 Heat the oil in a pan, add the onion and garlic and gently fry for about 5 minutes until softened.

2 Add the tomatoes, tomato purée, herbs, sugar and seasoning.

3 Simmer, uncovered, stirring occasionally for 15-20 minutes or until the tomatoes have reduced to a thick pulp. Leave to stand until the mixture is cool enough to spread on the pizza base.

Flavoured Oils

For extra flavour brush these tasty oils over the pizza base before adding the topping. The oil also forms a kind of protective seal that will help to keep the crust crisp and dry.

Chilli
150ml/¹⁄₄ pint/²⁄₃ cup olive oil
10ml/2 tsp tomato purée (paste)
15ml/1 tbsp dried red chilli flakes

1 Heat the oil, add the tomato purée and chilli flakes. Leave to cool.

2 Pour the chilli oil into a small jar or bottle. Stopper or cover and store in the fridge for up to 2 months (it gathers strength over time; the longer you keep it the hotter it gets).

Garlic
3–4 whole garlic cloves
120ml/4fl oz/¹⁄₂ cup olive oil

1 Peel the garlic cloves and put them into a small jar or bottle. Pour in the oil, cover and refrigerate for up to 1 month.

Margherita (Tomato, Basil and Mozzarella)

This classic pizza is very simple to prepare. The sweet flavour of sun-ripe tomatoes works wonderfully with the aromatic flavour of basil and the creamy mozzarella.

Serves 2–3

1 pizza base, about 25–30cm/10–12in
    diameter
30ml/2 tbsp olive oil
105ml/7 tbsp Tomato Sauce (*see* page 21)
150g/5oz mozzarella
2 ripe tomatoes, thinly sliced
6–8 fresh basil leaves
30ml/2 tbsp freshly grated Parmesan
black pepper

3 Arrange the sliced mozzarella and tomatoes on top of the pizza base.

4 Roughly tear the basil leaves, add and sprinkle with the Parmesan. Drizzle over the remaining oil. Bake for 15–20 minutes until crisp and golden. Serve at once.

1 Preheat the oven to 220°C/425°F/ Gas 7. Brush the base with 15ml/1 tbsp of the oil, then spread with tomato sauce.

2 Cut the mozzarella into thin slices.

Marinara (Tomato and Garlic)

The combination of garlic, good quality extra virgin olive oil and some chopped oregano adds an unmistakably Italian flavour to this simple pizza.

Serves 2–3

60ml/4 tbsp extra virgin olive oil
675g/1½lb plum tomatoes, peeled, seeded and chopped
1 pizza base, about 25–30cm/10–12in diameter
4 garlic cloves, cut into slivers
15ml/1 tbsp chopped fresh oregano
salt and black pepper

1 Preheat the oven to 220°C/425°F/ Gas 7. Heat 30ml/2 tbsp of the oil, add the tomatoes and cook for 5 minutes.

2 Place the tomatoes in a sieve and leave to drain for about 5 minutes.

3 Transfer the tomatoes to a food processor or blender and purée until the mixture is smooth. Brush the pizza base with half the remaining oil.

4 Spoon over the tomatoes and sprinkle with garlic and oregano. Drizzle with the remaining oil and season. Bake for 15–20 minutes until crisp and golden. Serve.

Quattro Stagioni (Four Seasons)

This traditional pizza is divided into quarters, each with a different topping: mushrooms, ham, olives and artichoke hearts, to depict the four seasons of the year.

Serves 2–4

45ml/3 tbsp olive oil
50g/2oz button mushrooms, sliced
1 pizza base, about 25–30cm/10–12in diameter
1 quantity Tomato Sauce (*see* page 21)
50g/2oz Parma ham
6 pitted black olives, chopped
4 bottled artichoke hearts in oil, drained
3 canned anchovy fillets, drained
50g/2oz mozzarella, thinly sliced
8 fresh basil leaves, shredded
black pepper

1 Preheat the oven to 220°C/425°F/Gas 7. Heat 15ml/1 tbsp of the oil in a frying pan and fry the mushrooms until all the juices have evaporated. Leave to cool.

2 Brush the pizza base with half the remaining oil. Spread over the tomato sauce and mark into four equal sections with a knife.

3 Arrange the mushrooms over one section of the pizza.

4 Cut the Parma ham into strips and arrange with the olives on another section of the pizza.

5 Thinly slice the artichoke hearts and arrange over a third section. Halve the anchovies lengthways and arrange with the mozzarella over the fourth section.

6 Scatter over the basil. Drizzle over the remaining oil and season with black pepper. Bake for 15–20 minutes until crisp and golden. Serve immediately.

COOK'S TIP

Look for buffalo milk mozzarella, it has a creamy, soft texture and a delicious taste. If you cannot find it, mozzarella made from cow's milk can be used instead.

Napoletana

This classic pizza is a speciality of Naples. Although it is one of the simplest pizzas to prepare, it uses a flavourful blend of ingredients, such as mozzarella, anchovies and Parmesan cheese.

3 Mix the mozzarella with the anchovies and scatter over the pizza base.

Serves 2–3

1 pizza base, about 25–30cm/10–12in diameter
30ml/2 tbsp olive oil
6 plum tomatoes
2 garlic cloves, chopped
115g/4oz mozzarella, grated
50g/2oz can anchovy fillets, drained and chopped
15ml/1 tbsp chopped fresh oregano
30ml/2 tbsp freshly grated Parmesan
black pepper

1 Preheat the oven to 220°C/425°F/ Gas 7. Brush the pizza base with 15ml/ 1 tbsp of the oil. Put the tomatoes in a bowl and pour over boiling water. Leave for 30 seconds, then plunge them into cold water.

2 Peel the tomatoes, remove the seeds then roughly chop them. Place the pizza base on a baking sheet, then spoon the chopped tomatoes over the pizza base, spreading it almost to the edge, and sprinkle over the garlic.

4 Sprinkle over the oregano and grated Parmesan. Drizzle over the remaining oil and season with ground black pepper. Bake the pizza for 15–20 minutes until the base is crisp and golden. Serve the pizza immediately.

COOK'S TIP
If you don't want to add anchovies to your pizza, try using 5ml/1 tsp capers instead. They add an interestingly tangy flavour to the topping.

Quattro Formaggi (Four Cheeses)

Rich and cheesy, these individual pizzas are quick to assemble, and the aroma of melting cheese is irresistible. Serve with a tossed green salad to balance the richness.

Serves 4

1 quantity Basic or Superquick
   Pizza Dough (*see* page 16)
15ml/1 tbsp Garlic Oil (*see* page 21)
1 small red onion, very thinly sliced
50g/2oz dolcelatte
50g/2oz mozzarella
50g/2oz Gruyère, grated
30ml/2 tbsp freshly grated Parmesan
15ml/1 tbsp chopped fresh thyme
black pepper

3 Mix together the Gruyère, Parmesan and thyme and sprinkle over.

4 Grind over plenty of black pepper. Bake for 15–20 minutes until crisp and golden and the cheese is bubbling. Serve at once.

1 Preheat the oven to 220°C/425°F/ Gas 7. Divide the dough into four pieces and roll out each one on a lightly floured surface into a 13cm/5 in circle.

2 Place well apart on two greased baking sheets, then push up the dough edges to make a thin rim. Brush with garlic oil and top with the red onion. Cut the dolcelatte and mozzarella into cubes and scatter over the bases.

Fiorentina

Spinach and an egg are the star ingredients of this pizza. A grating of nutmeg and a squeeze of lemon to heighten its flavour gives this pizza its unique character.

Serves 2–3

175g/6oz fresh spinach
45ml/3 tbsp olive oil
1 small red onion, thinly sliced
1 pizza base, about 25–30cm/
    10–12in diameter
1 quantity Tomato Sauce (*see* page 21)
freshly grated nutmeg
150g/5oz mozzarella
1 egg
25g/1oz Gruyère, grated

1 Preheat the oven to 220°C/425°F/ Gas 7. Remove the stalks from the spinach and wash the leaves in plenty of cold water. Drain well and pat dry with kitchen paper.

2 Heat 15 ml/1 tbsp of the oil and fry the onion until soft. Add the spinach and continue to fry until just wilted. Drain off any excess liquid.

3 Brush the pizza base with half the remaining oil. Spread over the tomato sauce, then top with the spinach mixture. Grate over some nutmeg.

4 Thinly slice the mozzarella and arrange over the spinach. Drizzle over the remaining oil. Bake for 10 minutes, then remove from the oven.

VARIATION
For an extra crunch, scatter over 30ml/ 2 tbsp sunflower seeds, sesame seeds or pine nuts just before baking.

5 Make a small well in the centre and drop in the egg.

6 Sprinkle over the Gruyère and return to the oven for a further 5–10 minutes until crisp and golden. Serve immediately.

American Hot

This popular pizza is spiced with green chillies and pepperoni and it is very versatile. If you prefer, use green olives and garnish with fresh basil leaves.

Serves 2–3

1 pizza base, about 25–30cm/10–12in diameter
15ml/1 tbsp olive oil
115g/4oz can peeled and chopped green chillies in brine, drained
1 quantity Tomato Sauce (*see* page 21)
75g/3oz sliced pepperoni
6 pitted black olives
15ml/1 tbsp chopped fresh oregano
115g/4oz mozzarella, grated
oregano leaves, to garnish

2 Brush the base with oil.

5 Sprinkle over the grated mozzarella and bake for 15–20 minutes until the pizza is crisp and golden.

1 Preheat the oven to 220°C/425°F/ Gas 7. Stir the chillies into the tomato sauce.

3 Spread with sauce; add the pepperoni.

6 Garnish with oregano leaves and serve immediately.

4 Halve the olives lengthways and scatter over, with the oregano.

VARIATION
You can make this pizza as hot as you like. For a really fiery version use fresh red or green chillies, cut into thin slices, in place of the chillies in brine.

Prosciutto, Mushroom and Artichoke

Here is a pizza full of rich and varied Italian flavours: Parmesan, prosciutto and artichokes. For a delicious variation, add a few varieties of cultivated mushrooms.

Serves 2–3

1 bunch spring onions (scallions)
60ml/4 tbsp olive oil
225g/8oz mushrooms, sliced
2 garlic cloves, chopped
1 pizza base, about 25–30cm/10–12in
   diameter
8 slices prosciutto di speck
4 bottled artichoke hearts in oil, drained
   and sliced
60ml/4 tbsp freshly grated Parmesan
salt and black pepper
thyme sprigs, to garnish

1 Preheat the oven to 220°C/425°F/ Gas 7. Trim the spring onions, then chop the white and some of the green stems.

2 Heat 30ml/2 tbsp of the oil in a frying pan. Add the spring onions, mushrooms and garlic and fry over a moderate heat until all the juices have evaporated. Season and leave to cool.

3 Brush the pizza base with half the remaining oil. Arrange the prosciutto, mushrooms and artichoke hearts on top.

4 Sprinkle over the Parmesan, then drizzle over the remaining oil and season. Bake for 15–20 minutes. Garnish with thyme sprigs and serve immediately.

Chorizo and Corn

The combination of spicy chorizo and sweet, tender corn works well in this hearty and colourful pizza. For a simple variation you could use chopped fresh basil instead of flat-leaf parsley.

Serves 2–3

1 pizza base, about 25–30cm/10–12in
    diameter
15ml/l tbsp Garlic Oil (*see* page 21)
1 quantity Tomato Sauce (*see* page 21)
175g/6oz chorizo sausages
175g/6oz (drained weight)
    canned corn
30ml/2 tbsp chopped fresh
    flat-leaf parsley (Italian parsley)
50g/2oz mozzarella, grated
30ml/2 tbsp freshly grated Parmesan

1 Preheat the oven to 220°C/425°F/ Gas 7. Brush the pizza base with garlic oil and spread over the tomato sauce.

2 Skin and cut the chorizo sausages into chunks and scatter over the tomato sauce. Bake for 10 minutes then remove from the oven.

COOK'S TIP
if you don't have chorizo, you can substitute pepperoni, which is an Italian-American spicy salami.

3 Sprinkle over the corn and flat-leaf parsley.

4 Mix together the mozzarella and Parmesan and sprinkle over. Bake for a further 5–10 minutes until crisp and golden. Serve immediately.

Chilli Beef

Ground beef, red kidney beans and smoky cheese combined with some aromatic chopped oregano, cumin and chillies give this pizza a delicious Mexican character.

Serves 4

30ml/2 tbsp olive oil
1 red onion, finely chopped
1 garlic clove, crushed
1 red (bell) pepper, seeded and chopped
175g/6oz lean minced (ground) beef
2.5ml/½ tsp ground cumin
2 fresh red chillies, seeded and chopped
115g/4oz (drained weight) canned red
    kidney beans
1 quantity Cornmeal Pizza Dough (*see*
    page 17)
1 quantity Tomato Sauce (*see* page 21)
15ml/1 tbsp chopped fresh oregano
50g/2oz mozzarella, grated
75g/3oz oak-smoked Cheddar, grated
salt and black pepper

1 Preheat the oven to 220°C/425°F/ Gas 7. Heat 15 ml/1 tbsp of the oil in a frying pan, add the onion, garlic and pepper and gently fry until soft. Increase the heat, add the beef and brown well,

2 Add the cumin and chillies and continue to cook, stirring, for about 5 minutes. Add the beans and seasoning.

3 Roll out the dough on a surface dusted with cornmeal and use to line a 30 x 18cm/12 x 7in greased Swiss-roll tin. Push up the dough edges to make a rim.

4 Spread over the tomato sauce.

VARIATION
If you prefer a milder version of this spicy pizza, reduce the amount of fresh chillies, or leave them out altogether.

5 Spoon over the beef mixture then scatter over the oregano.

6 Sprinkle over the cheeses and bake for 15–20 minutes until crisp and golden. Serve immediately.

Chicken and Shiitake Mushroom

The addition of shiitake mushrooms lends a distinctive rich smoky flavour to this colourful pizza, while a little fresh red chilli gives a hint of spiciness.

Serves 3–4

45ml/3 tbsp olive oil
350g/12oz chicken breast fillets, skinned and cut into thin strips
1 bunch spring onions (scallions), sliced
1 fresh red chilli, seeded and chopped
1 red (bell) pepper, seeded and cut into thin strips
75g/3oz fresh shiitake mushrooms, wiped and sliced
45–60ml/3–4 tbsp chopped fresh coriander (cilantro)
1 pizza base, about 25–30cm/10–12in diameter
15ml/1 tbsp Chilli Oil (*see* page 21)
150g/5oz mozzarella
salt and black pepper

1 Preheat the oven to 220°C/425°F/ Gas 7. Heat 30ml/2 tbsp of the olive oil in a wok or large frying pan. Add the chicken, spring onions, chilli, pepper and mushrooms and stir-fry over a high heat for 2–3 minutes until the chicken is firm but still slightly pink within. Season.

2 Pour off any excess oil, then set aside the chicken mixture to cool.

3 Add the fresh coriander to the chicken.

4 Brush the pizza base with the chilli oil.

5 Spoon over the chicken mixture and drizzle over the remaining olive oil.

6 Grate the mozzarella and sprinkle over. Bake for 15–20 minutes until crisp and golden. Serve immediately.

Pancetta, Leek and Smoked Mozzarella

With its topping of smoky-flavoured mozzarella, pancetta and leeks, this is an extremely tasty pizza that is easily prepared for a light lunch or supper.

Serves 4

30ml/2 tbsp freshly grated Parmesan
1 quantity Basic (*see* page 16) or
 Superquick Pizza Dough (*see* page 18)
30ml/2 tbsp olive oil
2 medium leeks
8–12 slices pancetta
150g/5oz smoked mozzarella
black pepper

1 Preheat the oven to 220°C/425°F/
Gas 7. Dust the work surface with the Parmesan, then knead into the dough. Divide the dough into four pieces and roll out each one to a 13cm/5in circle.

2 Place the circles of dough well apart on two greased baking sheets, then push up the edges to make a thin rim. Brush with 15ml/1 tbsp of the oil.

COOK'S TIP
Pancetta is a type of Italian bacon made from pork belly. It is unsmoked and cured in salt and a mixture of spices, then dried for a few months.

3 Trim and thinly slice the leeks into rounds. Arrange the pancetta and leeks over the pizza bases.

4 Grate the mozzarella and sprinkle over. Drizzle over the remaining oil and season with pepper. Bake for 15–20 minutes until crisp and golden. Serve immediately.

Ham and Mozzarella Calzone

A calzone is a kind of "inside-out" pizza – the dough is on the outside and the filling on the inside. For a vegetarian version replace the ham with mushrooms or chopped spinach.

Serves 2

1 quantity Basic (*see* page 16) or
   Superquick Pizza Dough (*see* page 18)
115g/4oz ricotta
30ml/2 tbsp freshly grated Parmesan
1 egg yolk
30ml/2 tbsp chopped fresh basil
75g/3oz cooked ham, finely chopped
75g/3oz mozzarella, cut into small cubes
olive oil for brushing
salt and black pepper

3 Spread the mixture over half of each circle, leaving a 2.5cm/1in border, then scatter the ham and mozzarella on top. Dampen the edges with water, then fold over the other half of dough to enclose the filling.

4 Press the edges firmly together to seal. Place on two greased baking sheets. Brush with oil and make a small hole in the top of each to allow the steam to escape. Bake for 15–20 minutes until golden. Serve immediately.

1 Preheat the oven to 220°C/425°F/ Gas 7. Divide the dough in half and roll out each piece on a lightly floured surface to an 18cm/7in circle.

2 In a bowl mix together the ricotta. Parmesan, egg yolk, basil and seasoning.

COOK'S TIP
Calzone are great for lunch boxes, as they were originally created to be 'food on the move'.

Smoked Chicken and Tomato Pizzettes

These ingredients complement each other perfectly and make a really delicious topping. The combination of basil, tomato paste and peppers produces a wonderful aroma.

Serves 4

1 quantity Basic (*see* page 16) or
    Superquick Pizza Dough (*see* page 18)
45ml/3 tbsp olive oil
60ml/4 tbsp sun-dried tomato paste
2 yellow (bell) peppers, seeded and cut
    into thin strips
175g/6oz sliced smoked chicken or
    turkey, chopped
150g/5oz mozzarella, cubed
30ml/2 tbsp chopped fresh basil
salt and black pepper

3 Stir-fry the peppers in half of the remaining oil for 3–4 minutes.

5 Scatter the mozzarella and basil among the four pizzas. Season with salt and ground black pepper.

1 Preheat the oven to 220°C/425°F/ Gas 7. Divide the dough into four pieces and roll out each one on a lightly floured surface to a 13cm/5in circle. Place well apart on two greased baking sheets, then push up the dough edges to make a thin rim. Brush with 15ml/1 tbsp of the oil.

2 Brush the pizza bases generously with the sun-dried tomato paste.

4 Arrange the chicken and peppers on top of the sun-dried tomato paste.

6 Drizzle over the remaining oil and bake for 15–20 minutes until crisp and golden. Serve immediately.

VARIATION
For a vegetarian pizza with a similar smoky taste, omit the chicken, roast the yellow peppers and remove the skins before using, and replace the mozzarella with Bavarian smoked cheese.

Spicy Sausage

This tasty pizza will make a substantial meal when served with a mixed salad and some vegetables. You can ring the changes by using chopped fresh basil and parsley.

Serves 3–4

225g/8oz good quality pork sausages
5ml/1tsp mild chilli powder
2.5ml/ ½ tsp freshly ground black pepper
30ml/2 tbsp olive oil
2–3 garlic cloves
1 pizza base, about 25–30cm/10–12in
    diameter
1 quantity Tomato Sauce (*see* page 21)
1 red onion, thinly sliced
15ml/1 tbsp chopped fresh oregano
15ml/1 tbsp chopped fresh thyme
50g/2oz mozzarella, grated
50g/2oz freshly grated Parmesan

1 Preheat the oven to 220°C/425°F/Gas 7. Skin the sausages by running a sharp knife down the side of the skins. Place the sausagemeat in a bowl and add the chilli powder and black pepper; mix well. Break the sausagemeat into walnut-sized balls.

2 Heat 15ml/1 tbsp of the oil in a frying pan and fry the sausage balls for 2–3 minutes until evenly browned.

3 Using a slotted spoon remove the sausage balls from the pan and drain on kitchen paper.

4 Thinly slice the garlic cloves.

5 Brush the pizza base with the remaining oil, then spread over the tomato sauce. Scatter over the sausages, garlic, onion and the fresh herbs.

6 Sprinkle over the mozzarella and Parmesan and bake for 15–20 minutes until crisp and golden. Serve immediately.

COOK'S TIP
This pizza would be delicious made with fresh Italian spicy sausages, available from good delicatessens.

Onion, Salami and Black Olive

With its topping of sweet caramelized onions, salty black olives, herbes de Provence and a sprinkling of Parmesan, this pizza is extremely flavoursome.

Serves 4

700g/1½lb red onions
60ml/4 tbsp olive oil
12 pitted black olives
1 quantity Basic (*see* page 16) or
   Superquick Pizza Dough (*see* page 18)
5ml/1tsp dried herbes de Provence
6–8 slices Italian salami, quartered
30–45ml/2–3 tbsp freshly
   grated Parmesan
black pepper

1 Preheat the oven to 220°C/425°F/ Gas 7. Thinly slice the onions.

2 Heat 30ml/2 tbsp of the oil in a pan and add the onions. Cover and cook gently for 15–20 minutes, stirring occasionally until the onions are soft and lightly browned. Leave to cool.

COOK'S TIP
Make more caramelized onions than you need and freeze them in separate portions. Use for salads, pizzas, sandwiches and pasta dishes.

3 Finely chop the black olives.

4 Knead the dough and add the black olives and herbes de Provence. Roll out the dough and line a 30 x18cm/12 x 7in Swiss-roll tin. Push edges up to make a rim and brush with half the remaining oil.

5 Spoon on half the onions, top with the salami slices and the remaining onions.

6 Grind over plenty of black pepper and drizzle over the remaining oil. Bake for 15–20 minutes until crisp and golden. Remove from the oven and sprinkle over the Parmesan to serve.

Ham and Pineapple French Bread Pizza

French bread makes a great pizza base when you need to produce a tasty snack or light lunch quickly. Instead of ham, you could use a can of tuna from the storecupboard.

Serves 4

2 small baguettes
1 quantity Tomato Sauce (*see* page 21)
75 g/3 oz sliced cooked ham
4 rings canned pineapple, drained well
    and chopped
1 small green (bell) pepper, seeded and
    cut into thin strips
75 g/3 oz mature Cheddar
salt and black pepper

COOK'S TIP
For a change use focaccia or ciabatta instead of the baguettes.

1 Preheat the oven to 200°C/400°F/ Gas 6. Cut the baguettes in half and toast the cut sides until they are crisp and golden brown.

2 Spread the tomato sauce over the toasted baguettes.

3 Cut the ham into strips and arrange on the baguettes with the pineapple and pepper. Season.

4 Grate the Cheddar and sprinkle on top. Bake or grill for 15–20 minutes until crisp and golden.

Ham, Pepper and Mozzarella Pizzas

Succulent roasted peppers, salty Parma ham, basil, and creamy mozzarella – the delicious flavours of these easy ciabatta pizzas are hard to beat.

Serves 2

1 ciabatta
1 red (bell) pepper, roasted and peeled
1 yellow (bell) pepper, roasted and peeled
4 slices Parma ham, cut into thick strips
75g/3oz mozzarella
black pepper
tiny basil leaves, to garnish

1 Cut the ciabatta bread into four thick slices and toast both sides until golden.

2 Cut the roasted peppers into thick strips and arrange on the toasted bread with the Parma ham.

3 Thinly slice the mozzarella and arrange on top. Grind over plenty of black pepper. Place under a hot grill for 2–3 minutes until the cheese is bubbling.

4 Arrange the basil leaves on top and serve immediately.

Pepperoni Pan Pizza

This pizza is made using a scone base which does not need proving (time to rise). Choose whichever topping you prefer – prawns, ham or salami are all good alternatives to pepperoni.

Serves 2–3

15ml/1 tbsp chopped fresh mixed herbs
1 quantity Scone Pizza Dough (*see* page 18)
30ml/2 tbsp tomato purée (paste)
400g/14oz can chopped tomatoes, drained well
50g/2oz button mushrooms, thinly sliced
75g/3oz sliced pepperoni
6 pitted black olives, chopped
50g/2oz Edam, grated
50g/2oz mature Cheddar, grated
15ml/1 tbsp chopped fresh basil, to garnish

1 Add the herbs to the scone mix before mixing to a soft dough.

2 Turn the dough on to a lightly floured surface and knead lightly until smooth. Roll out to fit a well-greased frying pan, about 23cm/9in in diameter.

3 Cook the dough in the pan over a low heat for about 5 minutes until the base is golden. Lift carefully with a palette knife to check.

4 Turn the base on to a baking sheet, then slide it back into the pan, with the cooked side uppermost.

5 Mix together the tomato purée and drained tomatoes and spread over the pizza base. Scatter over the mushrooms, pepperoni, olives and cheeses. Continue to cook for about 5 minutes until the underside is golden.

6 When it is ready, transfer the pan to a preheated moderate grill for 4–5 minutes. Scatter over the basil and serve.

COOK'S TIP
If you are short of time, this pizza is perfect. It is so easy to make that you could get children to help you make it, and choose their own toppings, too.

Mixed Seafood

Here is a pizza that gives you the full flavour of the Mediterranean, ideal for a summer evening supper! Take care not to overcook the seafood or it will toughen up.

Serves 3–4

1 pizza base, 25–30cm/10–12in diameter
30ml/2 tbsp olive oil
1 quantity Tomato Sauce (*see* page 21)
400g/14oz bag frozen mixed cooked
    seafood (including mussels, prawns
    (shrimp) and squid), defrosted
3 garlic cloves
30ml/2 tbsp chopped fresh parsley
30ml/2 tbsp freshly grated Parmesan,
    to garnish

1 Preheat the oven to 220°C/425°F/Gas 7. Brush the pizza base with 15ml/1 tbsp of the oil.

2 Spread over the Tomato Sauce. Bake for 10 minutes. Remove from the oven.

3 Pat the seafood dry using kitchen paper, then arrange on top.

4 Chop the garlic and scatter over.

5 Sprinkle the parsley all over the pizza, then drizzle with the remaining oil. Return to the oven.

6 Bake for a further 5–10 minutes until the seafood is warmed through and the base is crisp and golden. Sprinkle with Parmesan and serve immediately.

VARIATION
If you prefer, this pizza can be made with mussels or prawns (shrimp) on their own, or any combination of your favourite seafood.

Salmon and Avocado

Smoked and fresh salmon make a delicious pizza topping when mixed with avocado. Smoked salmon trimmings are cheaper than smoked salmon slices and could be used instead.

Serves 3–4

150g/5oz salmon fillet
120ml/4fl oz/½ cup dry white wine
1 pizza base, 25–30cm/10–12in diameter
15ml/1 tbsp olive oil
400g/14oz can chopped tomatoes,
    drained well
115g/4oz mozzarella, grated
1 small avocado
10ml/2 tsp lemon juice
30ml/2 tbsp crème fraîche
75g/3oz smoked salmon, cut into strips
15ml/1 tbsp capers
30ml/2 tbsp snipped fresh chives,
    to garnish
black pepper

1 Preheat the oven to 220°C/425°F/Gas 7. Place the salmon fillet in a frying pan, pour over the wine and season with black pepper. Bring slowly to the boil, remove from the heat, cover and cool. (The fish will cook in the cooling liquid.) Skin and flake the salmon into small pieces, removing any bones.

2 Brush the pizza base with the oil and spread over the tomatoes. Sprinkle over 50g/2 oz of the mozzarella. Bake for 10 minutes, then remove from the oven.

3 Meanwhile, halve, stone and peel the avocado. Cut the flesh into small cubes and toss carefully in the lemon juice.

4 Dot teaspoonsful of the crème fraîche over the pizza base.

VARIATION

Smoked trout or mackerel would be equally good on this pizza; sprinkle with a little lemon juice before use.

5 Arrange the fresh and smoked salmon, avocado, capers and remaining mozzarella on top. Season with black pepper. Bake for a further 5–10 minutes until crisp and golden.

6 Sprinkle over the chives and serve.

Prawn, Sun-dried Tomato and Basil

Sun-dried tomatoes with their concentrated caramelized tomato flavour make an excellent topping for pizzas. Serve these pretty pizzettes as an appetizer or snack.

2 Roll out each one on a lightly floured surface to a small oval about 5mm/¼in thick. Place well apart on two greased baking sheets. Prick all over with a fork.

3 Brush the pizza bases with 15ml/1 tbsp of the chilli oil and top with the mozzarella, leaving a 1cm/½in border.

Serves 4

1 quantity Basic (*see* page 16) or
   Superquick Pizza Dough (*see* page 18)
30ml/2 tbsp Chilli Oil
75g/3oz mozzarella, grated
1 garlic clove, chopped
1 small red onion, thinly sliced
4–6 pieces sun-dried tomatoes,
   thinly sliced
115g/4oz cooked prawns (shrimp), peeled
30ml/2 tbsp chopped fresh basil
salt and black pepper
shredded basil leaves, to garnish

1 Preheat the oven to 220°C/425°F/Gas 7. Divide the dough into eight pieces.

4 Divide the garlic, onion, sun dried tomatoes, prawns and basil between the pizza bases. Season and drizzle over the remaining chilli oil. Bake for 8–10 minutes until crisp and golden. Garnish with basil leaves and serve immediately.

Crab and Parmesan Calzonelli

These miniature calzone owe their popularity to their impressive presentation. As in Italy, these are portable pizzas, so would be ideal for a packed lunch or picnic.

Makes 10–12

1 quantity Basic (*see* page 16) or
    Superquick Pizza Dough (*see* page 18)
115g/4oz mixed prepared crab meat,
    defrosted if frozen
15ml/1 tbsp double (heavy) cream
30ml/2 tbsp freshly grated Parmesan
30ml/2 tbsp chopped fresh parsley
1 garlic clove, crushed
salt and black pepper
parsley sprigs, to garnish

1 Preheat the oven to 200°C/400°F/Gas 6. Roll out the dough on a lightly floured surface to 3mm/⅛in thick. Using a 7.5cm/3in plain round cutter stamp out 10–12 circles.

2 In a bowl mix together the crab meat, cream, Parmesan, parsley, garlic and seasoning.

VARIATIONS

If you prefer, use white crab meat instead of mixed, and chopped fresh coriander (cilantro) in place of the parsley.

3 Spoon a little of the filling on to one half of each circle. Dampen the edges with water and fold over to enclose filling. Lightly press the edges together.

4 Seal the edges by pressing with a fork. Place well apart on two greased baking sheets. Bake for 10–15 minutes until golden. Garnish with parsley sprigs.

Mussel and Leek Pizzettes

Serve these tasty seafood pizzettes accompanied by a crisp green salad for a light lunch or supper. This pizza would work equally well with fresh baby clams.

Serves 4

450g/1lb live mussels
120ml/4fl oz/½ cup dry white wine
1 quantity Basic (*see* page 16) or
    Superquick Pizza Dough (*see* page 18)
15ml/1 tbsp olive oil
50g/2oz Gruyère
50g/2oz mozzarella
2 small leeks
salt and black pepper

1 Preheat the oven to 220°C/425°F/Gas 7. Place the mussels in a bowl of cold water to soak, and scrub well. Remove the beards and discard any mussels that remain open when sharply tapped.

2 Place the mussels in a pan. Pour over the wine, cover and cook over a high heat, shaking the pan occasionally, for 5–10 minutes until the mussels have opened.

3 Drain off the cooking liquid. Remove the mussels from their shells, discarding any that remain closed. Leave to cool.

VARIATION
Frozen or canned mussels can also be used, but will not have the same flavour and texture. Make sure you defrost the mussels properly.

4 Divide the dough into four pieces and roll out each one on a lightly floured surface to a 13cm/5in circle. Place well apart on two greased baking sheets, then push up the dough to form a thin rim. Brush the pizza bases with oil. Grate the cheeses and sprinkle half over the bases.

5 Thinly slice the leeks, then scatter over the cheese. Bake for 10 minutes, then remove from the oven.

6 Arrange the mussels on top. Season and sprinkle over the remaining cheese. Bake for a further 5–10 minutes until crisp and golden. Serve immediately.

Anchovy, Pepper and Tomato

This pretty, summery pizza is simple to make, yet quite delicious. It's well worth grilling the peppers as they take on a lovely smoky flavour.

Serves 2–3

6 plum tomatoes
45ml/3 tbsp olive oil
5ml/1tsp salt
1 large red (bell) pepper
1 large yellow (bell) pepper
1 pizza base, 25–30cm/10–12in diameter
2 garlic cloves, chopped
50g/2oz can anchovy fillets, drained
black pepper
basil leaves, to garnish

1 Halve the tomatoes lengthways and scoop out the seeds.

2 Roughly chop the flesh and place in a bowl with 15 ml/1 tbsp of the oil and the salt. Mix well, then leave to marinate for 30 minutes.

COOK'S TIP
This pizza would look very appealing when served with a mixed green salad of rocket (arugula), watercress, cucumber and beansprouts.

3 Meanwhile, preheat the oven to 220°C/425°F/Gas 7. Slice the peppers in half lengthways and remove the seeds. Place the pepper halves, skin-side up, on a baking sheet and grill until the skins are evenly charred.

4 Place the peppers in a covered bowl for 10 minutes, then peel off the skins. Cut the flesh into thin strips.

5 Brush the pizza base with half the remaining oil. Drain the tomatoes, then scatter over the base with the peppers and garlic.

6 Snip the anchovy fillets into small pieces and sprinkle over the pizza. Season with black pepper. Drizzle over the remaining oil and bake for 15–20 minutes until crisp and golden. Garnish with basil leaves and serve immediately.

Tuna, Anchovy and Caper

This simple tuna pizza is enhanced by the lovely Mediterranean flavours of capers, black olives, Parmesan and anchovies. Just add a simple salad for a perfect meal.

Serves 2–3

1 quantity Scone Pizza Dough (*see* page 18)
30ml/2 tbsp olive oil
1 quantity Tomato Sauce (*see* page 21)
1 small red onion
200g/7oz can tuna, drained
15ml/1 tbsp capers
12 pitted black olives
45ml/3 tbsp freshly grated Parmesan
50g/2oz can anchovy fillets, drained and halved lengthways

3 Roughly flake the tuna with a fork and scatter over the onion.

4 Sprinkle over the capers, black olives and Parmesan.

5 Place the anchovy fillets over the top of the pizza so that they form a lattice design.

1 Preheat the oven to 220°C/425°F/Gas 7. Roll out the dough on a lightly floured surface to a 25cm/10in circle. Place on a greased baking sheet and brush with 15ml/1 tbsp of the oil. Spread the tomato sauce evenly over the dough.

2 Cut the onion into thin wedges and arrange on top.

6 Drizzle over the remaining oil, then grind over plenty of black pepper. Bake for 15–20 minutes until crisp and golden. Serve immediately.

COOK'S TIP
Vary the topping by adding 1 sliced red (bell) pepper and 2 sliced sweet tomatoes, plus 15ml/1 tbsp chopped fresh basil.

Roasted Vegetable and Goat's Cheese

Here is a pizza which combines the smoky flavours of oven-roasted vegetables, tangy green tapenade, garlic oil and the distinctive taste of goat's cheese.

Serves 3

1 aubergine (eggplant), cut into
    thick chunks
2 small courgettes (zucchini), sliced
1 red (bell) pepper, quartered and seeded
1 yellow (bell) pepper, quartered
    and seeded
1 small red onion, cut into wedges
90ml/6 tbsp Garlic Oil (*see page 21*)
1 pizza base, 25–30cm/10–12in diameter
1 x 400g/14oz can chopped tomatoes,
    drained well
1 x 115g/4oz goat's cheese (with rind)
15ml/1 tbsp chopped fresh thyme
green olive tapenade

1 Preheat the oven to 220°C/425°F/Gas 7. Place the aubergine, courgettes, peppers and onion in a large roasting tin. Brush with 60ml/4 tbsp of the garlic oil. Roast for about 30 minutes until lightly charred, turning the peppers half-way through cooking. Remove from the oven and set aside.

2 When the peppers are cool enough to handle, peel off the skins and cut the flesh into thick strips.

3 Brush the pizza base with half the remaining garlic oil and spread over the drained tomatoes.

4 Arrange the roasted vegetables on top of the pizza.

COOK'S TIP
If you place the roasted peppers in a plastic bag while they cool, peeling off the skins becomes easier.

5 Cube the goat's cheese and arrange on top. Scatter over the thyme.

6 Drizzle over the remaining garlic oil and season with black pepper. Bake for 15–20 minutes until crisp and golden. Spoon the tapenade over to serve.

New Potato, Rosemary and Garlic

New potatoes, smoked mozzarella, rosemary and garlic make the flavour of this pizza unique.
For a delicious variation, use sage instead of rosemary.

Serves 2–3

350g/12 oz new potatoes
45ml/3 tbsp olive oil
2 garlic cloves, crushed
1 pizza base, 25–30cm/10–12in diameter
1 red onion, thinly sliced
150g/5oz smoked mozzarella, grated
10ml/2tsp chopped fresh rosemary
salt and black pepper
30ml/2 tbsp freshly grated Parmesan,
      to garnish

1 Preheat the oven to 200°C/425°F/
Gas 7. Cook the potatoes for 5 minutes.
Drain well. Cool, peel and slice thinly.

2 Heat 30ml/2 tbsp of the oil in a frying
pan. Add the sliced potatoes and garlic
and fry for 5–8 minutes until tender.

3 Brush the pizza base with the remaining
oil. Scatter over the onion, then arrange
the potatoes on top.

4 Sprinkle over the grated mozzarella and
fresh rosemary. Grind over plenty of black
pepper and bake for 15–20 minutes until
the topping is crisp and golden. Remove
from the oven and sprinkle over the
Parmesan to serve.

Wild Mushroom Pizzettes

Serve these pizzas as a starter. Fresh wild mushrooms add distinctive flavour to the topping but cultivated mushrooms such as shiitake, oyster and chestnut mushrooms would do just as well.

Serves 4

45ml/3 tbsp olive oil
350g/12oz fresh wild mushrooms, washed
    and sliced
2 shallots, chopped
2 garlic cloves, finely chopped
30ml/2 tbsp chopped fresh mixed thyme
    and flat-leaf parsley
1 quantity Basic (*see* page 16) or
    Superquick Pizza Dough (*see* page 18)
40g/1½oz Gruyère, grated
30ml/2 tbsp freshly grated Parmesan
salt and black pepper

1 Preheat the oven to 220°C/425°F/ Gas 7. Heat 30ml/2 tbsp of the oil in a large frying pan. Add the mushrooms, shallots and garlic and fry over a moderate heat until all the juices have evaporated.

2 Stir in half the herbs and seasoning, then set aside to cool. Divide the dough into four and roll out each piece on a lightly floured surface to form a 13cm/ 5in circle.

3 Place well apart on two greased baking sheets, then push up the dough edges to form a thin rim. Brush the pizza bases with the remaining oil and top with the wild mushroom mixture.

4 Mix together the Gruyère and Parmesan, then sprinkle over. Bake for 15–20 minutes until crisp and golden. Remove from the oven and scatter over the remaining herbs to serve.

Chilli, Tomatoes and Spinach

This richly flavoured topping with a hint of fire, some smoky cheese and chopped green spinach makes a colourful and satisfying pizza.

Serves 3

1–2 fresh red chillies
45ml/3 tbsp tomato oil (from jar of sun-dried tomatoes)
1 onion, chopped
2 garlic cloves, chopped
50g/2oz (drained weight) sun-dried tomatoes in oil
400g/14oz can chopped tomatoes
15ml/1 tbsp tomato purée
175g/6oz fresh spinach
1 pizza base, 25–30cm/10–12in diameter
75g/3oz smoked Bavarian cheese, grated
75g/3oz mature Cheddar, grated
salt and black pepper

1 Seed and finely chop the chillies.

2 Heat 30ml/2 tbsp of the tomato oil in a pan, add the onion, garlic and chillies and gently fry for about 5 minutes until they are soft.

3 Roughly chop the sun-dried tomatoes. Add to the pan with the chopped tomatoes, tomato purée and seasoning. Simmer uncovered, stirring occasionally, for 15 minutes.

4 Remove the stalks from the spinach and wash the leaves in plenty of cold water. Drain well and pat dry with kitchen paper. Roughly chop the spinach.

COOK'S TIP
Instead of spinach, you can use chicory (Belgian endive), rocket (arugula), kale, or Swiss chard.

5 Stir the spinach into the sauce. Cook, stirring, for a further 5–10 minutes until the spinach has wilted and no excess moisture remains. Leave to cool.

6 Meanwhile, preheat the oven to 220°C/425°F/Gas 7. Brush the pizza base with the remaining tomato oil, then spoon over the sauce. Sprinkle over the cheeses and bake for 15–20 minutes until crisp and golden. Serve immediately.

Tomato, Pesto and Black Olive

These individual pizzas take very little time to put together. Marinating the tomatoes with a little crushed garlic and oil gives them extra flavour.

2 Meanwhile, preheat the oven to 220°C/425°F/Gas 7. Divide the dough into four and roll out each piece on a lightly floured surface to a 13cm/5in circle. Place well apart on two greased baking sheets, and push up the dough edges to make a rim. Brush with half the remaining oil and spread with pesto.

Serves 4

2 plum tomatoes
1 garlic clove, crushed
60ml/4 tbsp olive oil
1 quantity Basic (see page 16) or
    Superquick Pizza Dough (see page 18)
30ml/2 tbsp red pesto
150g/5oz mozzarella, thinly sliced
4 pitted black olives, chopped
15ml/1 tbsp chopped fresh oregano
salt and black pepper
oregano leaves, to garnish

1 Slice the tomatoes thinly crossways, then cut each slice in half. Place the tomatoes in a shallow dish with the garlic. Drizzle over 30ml/2 tbsp of the oil and season. Leave to marinate for 15 minutes.

3 Drain the tomatoes, then arrange slices of tomatoes and mozzarella on each base.

4 Sprinkle over the olives and oregano. Drizzle over the remaining oil and bake for 15–20 minutes until crisp and golden. Garnish with oregano leaves and serve.

Fresh Herb

Cut this pizza into thin wedges and serve as part of a mixed antipasti. With its mixture of chopped herbs, it has a deliciously fresh flavour.

Serves 8

115g/4oz mixed fresh herbs, such as
    parsley, basil and oregano
3 garlic cloves, crushed
120ml/4fl oz/½ cup double
    (heavy) cream
1 pizza base, 25–30cm/10–12in diameter
15ml/1 tbsp Garlic Oil (*see* page 21)
115g/4oz Pecorino, grated
salt and black pepper

3 Brush the pizza base with the garlic oil, then spread over the herb mixture.

4 Sprinkle over the Pecorino and bake for 15–20 minutes until crisp and golden. Cut into thin wedges and serve immediately.

1 Preheat the oven to 220°C/425°F/Gas 7. Chop the herbs, in a food processor.

2 In a bowl mix together the herbs, garlic, cream and seasoning.

Vegetable Calzone

Aubergines, shallots and sun-dried tomatoes make an unusual filling for calzone. Add more or less red chilli flakes, depending on personal taste.

Serves 2

45ml/3 tbsp olive oil
4 baby aubergines (eggplants)
3 shallots, chopped
1 garlic clove, chopped
50g/2oz (drained weight) sun-dried
    tomatoes in oil, chopped
1.25ml/¼ tsp dried red chilli flakes
10ml/2tsp chopped fresh thyme
1 quantity Basic (*see* page 16) or
    Superquick Pizza Dough (*see* page 18)
75g/3oz mozzarella, cubed
salt and black pepper
15–30ml/1–2 tbsp freshly grated
    Parmesan, to serve

1 Preheat the oven to 220°C/425°F/Gas 7. Trim the aubergines, then cut into small cubes.

2 Heat 15ml/1tbsp oil in a frying pan and cook the shallots until soft. Add the aubergines, garlic, sun-dried tomatoes, red chilli flakes, thyme and seasoning. Cook for 4–5 minutes, stirring frequently, until the aubergine is beginning to soften.

3 Divide the dough in half and roll out each piece on a lightly floured surface to an 18cm/7in circle.

4 Spread the aubergine mixture over half of each circle, leaving a 2.5cm/1in border, then scatter over the mozzarella.

COOK'S TIP
If you prefer, you could roast the vegetables in the oven before filling the pizza. Toss in 30ml/2 tbsp olive oil then roast in the preheated oven for 15–20 minutes.

5 Dampen the edges with water, then fold over the other half of dough to enclose the filling. Press the edges firmly together to seal. Place on two greased baking sheets.

6 Brush with half the remaining oil and make a small hole in the top of each to allow the steam to escape. Bake for 15–20 minutes until golden. Remove from the oven and brush with the remaining oil. Sprinkle over the Parmesan and serve immediately.

Tomato, Fennel and Parmesan

This pizza relies on the winning combination of tomatoes, fennel and Parmesan. The fennel adds both a crisp texture and a distinctive flavour.

Serves 2–3

1 fennel bulb, trimmed and quartered
    lengthways
45ml/3 tbsp Garlic Oil (*see* page 21)
1 pizza base 25–30cm/10–12in
    diameter
1 quantity Tomato Sauce (*see* page 21)
30ml/2 tbsp chopped fresh
    flat-leaf parsley
50g/2oz mozzarella, grated
50g/2oz Parmesan, grated
salt and black pepper

1 Preheat the oven to 220°C/425°F/Gas 7. Remove the fennel core and slice thinly.

2 Heat 30ml/2 tbsp of the garlic oil in a frying pan and sauté the fennel for 4–5 minutes until just tender. Season.

3 Brush the pizza base with the remaining garlic oil and spread over the tomato sauce. Spoon the fennel on top and scatter over the flat-leaf parsley.

4 Mix together the mozzarella and Parmesan and sprinkle over. Bake for 15–20 minutes until crisp and golden. Serve immediately.

COOK'S TIP
If you are short of time, you can buy both cheeses ready-grated.

Red Onion, Gorgonzola and Sage

This topping combines the richness of Gorgonzola with the earthy flavours of sage and sweet red onions, and a dash of Garlic Oil.

Serves 4

1 quantity Basic (*see* page 16) or
   Superquick Pizza Dough (*see* page 18)
30ml/2 tbsp Garlic Oil (*see* page 21)
2 small red onions
150g/5oz Gorgonzola piccante
2 garlic cloves, cut into thin strips
10ml/2tsp chopped fresh sage
black pepper

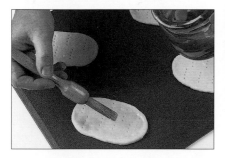

1 Preheat the oven to 220°C/425°F/Gas 7. Divide the dough into eight pieces and roll out each one on a lightly floured surface to a small oval about 5mm/¼in thick. Place well apart on two greased baking sheets and prick with a fork. Brush the bases well with 15ml/1 tbsp of the garlic oil.

2 Halve, then slice the onions into thin wedges. Scatter over the pizza bases.

COOK'S TIP
If you like a milder flavour, substitute another Italian blue cheese for the Gorgonzola. Dolcelatte would work well.

3 Remove the rind from the Gorgonzola. Cut the cheese into small cubes, then scatter it over the onions.

4 Sprinkle the garlic and sage onto the base. Drizzle the remaining oil on top and add black pepper. Bake for 10–15 minutes until crisp and golden. Serve immediately.

Onion and Three Cheese

You can use any combination of cheese you like. Edam and Cheddar work well on a pizza since they both have good flavours and melting properties.

2 Brush the pizza base with the remaining oil. Spoon over the onions and tomatoes, then scatter over the basil.

3 Thinly slice the cheeses and arrange over the tomatoes and onions.

4 Grind over plenty of black pepper and bake for 15-20 minutes until crisp and golden. Garnish with basil leaves, slice and serve immediately.

Serves 3-4

45ml/3 tbsp olive oil
3 medium onions, sliced
1 pizza base 25–30cm/10–12in
    diameter
4 small tomatoes, peeled, seeded and cut
    into thin wedges
30ml/2 tbsp chopped fresh basil
115g/4oz Dolcelatte
150g/5oz mozzarella
115g/4oz Red Leicester
black pepper
fresh basil leaves, to garnish

1 Preheat the oven to 220°C/425°F/Gas 7. Heat 30 ml/2 tbsp of the oil and gently fry the onions for about 10 minutes. Cool.

COOK'S TIP
Red onions would look equally appealing on this tasty pizza.

Feta, Roasted Garlic and Oregano

This is a pizza for anyone who loves garlic! Mash down the cloves as you eat – they should be soft and will have lost most of their pungency.

Serves 4

1 medium garlic bulb, unpeeled
45ml/3 tbsp olive oil
1 medium red (bell) pepper, quartered
    and seeded
1 medium yellow (bell) pepper, quartered
    and seeded
2 plum tomatoes
1 quantity Basic (*see* page 16) or
    Superquick Pizza Dough (*see* page 18)
175g/6oz feta, crumbled
black pepper
15–30ml/1–2 tbsp chopped fresh
    oregano, to garnish

1 Preheat the oven to 220°C/425°F/Gas 7. Break the garlic into cloves, discarding the outer papery layers. Toss in 15ml/ 1 tbsp of the oil.

2 Place the peppers skin-side up on a baking sheet and grill until the skins are evenly charred. Place in a covered bowl for 10 minutes, then peel off the skins. Cut the flesh into strips. Put the tomatoes in a bowl and pour over boiling water. Leave for 30 seconds, then plunge into cold water. Peel, seed and roughly chop the flesh.

3 Divide the dough into four pieces and roll out each one on a lightly floured surface to a 13cm/5in circle.

4 Place the dough circles well apart on two greased baking sheets, then push up the dough edges to form a thin rim. Brush with half the remaining oil and scatter over the chopped tomatoes. Top with the peppers, crumbled feta and garlic cloves. Drizzle over the remaining oil and season with black pepper.

5 Bake in the preheated oven for 15–20 minutes until crisp and golden. Garnish with chopped oregano and serve immediately.

Spring Vegetable and Pine Nuts

This colourful pizza is well worth the time it takes to prepare. You can vary the ingredients according to the season and their availability.

Serves 2–3

1 pizza base, 25–30cm/10–12in
 diameter
45 ml/3 tbsp Garlic Oil (*see* page 21)
1 quantity Tomato Sauce (*see* page 21)
4 spring onions (scallions)
2 courgettes (zucchini)
1 leek
115 g/4 oz asparagus tips
15 ml/1 tbsp chopped fresh oregano
30 ml/2 tbsp pine nuts
50 g/2 oz mozzarella, grated
30 ml/2 tbsp freshly grated Parmesan
black pepper

1 Preheat the oven to 220°C/425°F/Gas 7. Brush the pizza base with 15ml/1 tbsp of the garlic oil, then spread over the tomato sauce.

2 Slice the spring onions, courgettes, leek and asparagus.

3 Heat half the remaining garlic oil in a frying pan and stir-fry the vegetables for 3–5 minutes.

4 Arrange the vegetables over the tomato sauce.

5 Sprinkle the oregano and pine nuts over the pizza.

6 Mix together the mozzarella and Parmesan and sprinkle over the pizza. Drizzle over the remaining garlic oil and season with black pepper. Bake for 15–20 minutes until crisp and golden. Serve immediately.

COOK'S TIP
Fresh garden peas, cherry tomatoes and a mix of yellow, red and green (bell) peppers would be good additions to this pizza.

Spinach and Ricotta Panzerotti

Panzerotti are small pastries that are filled, then deep fried. They make great party food to serve with drinks or as tasty appetizers for a crowd.

Makes 20–24

115g/4oz frozen chopped spinach,
    defrosted and squeezed dry
50g/2oz ricotta
50g/2oz freshly grated Parmesan
generous pinch freshly grated nutmeg
2 quantities Basic (*see* page 16) or
    Superquick Pizza Dough (*see* page 18)
1 egg white, lightly beaten
vegetable oil for deep-frying
salt and black pepper

1 Place the spinach, ricotta, Parmesan, nutmeg and seasoning in a bowl and beat until smooth.

2 Roll out the dough on a lightly floured surface to about 3mm/⅛in thick. Using a 7.5cm/3in plain round cutter stamp out 20–24 circles.

COOK'S TIP
Do serve these as soon as possible after frying, they will become much less appetizing if left to cool.

3 Spread a teaspoonful of spinach mixture over one half of each circle.

4 Brush the edges of the dough with a little egg white.

5 Fold the dough over the filling and press the edges firmly together to seal.

6 Heat the oil in a large heavy-based pan or deep-fat fryer to 180°C/350°F. Deep-fry the panzerotti a few at a time for 2–3 minutes until golden. Drain on kitchen paper and serve immediately.

Smoked Salmon Pizzettes

Mini pizzas topped with smoked salmon, crème fraîche and lumpfish roe are always popular and make an extra special party canapé.

Makes 10–12

1 quantity Basic (*see* page 16) or
   Superquick Pizza Dough (*see* page 18)
15ml/1 tbsp snipped fresh chives
15ml/1 tbsp olive oil
75–115g/3–4oz smoked salmon, cut
   into strips
60ml/4 tbsp crème fraîche
30ml/2 tbsp black lumpfish roe
chives, to garnish

1 Preheat the oven to 200°C/400°F/Gas 6. Knead the dough gently, adding the chives until evenly mixed.

2 Roll out the dough on a lightly floured surface to about 3mm/⅛in thick. Using a 7.5cm/3in plain round cutter stamp out 10–12 circles.

3 Place the bases well apart on two greased baking sheets, prick all over with a fork, then brush with the oil. Bake for 10–15 minutes until crisp and golden.

4 Arrange the smoked salmon on top, then spoon on the crème fraîche. Spoon a tiny amount of lumpfish roe in the centre and garnish with chives. Serve immediately.

Tomato, Basil and Olive Pizza Bites

This quick and easy recipe uses scone pizza dough with the addition of chopped fresh basil. The combination of sun-dried tomatoes and basil leaves gives an intense, aromatic flavour.

Makes 24

18–20 fresh basil leaves
1 quantity Scone Pizza Dough (*see* page 18)
30ml/2 tbsp tomato oil (from jar of sun-dried tomatoes)
1 quantity Tomato Sauce (*see* page 21)
115g/4oz (drained weight) sun-dried tomatoes in oil, chopped
10 pitted black olives, chopped
50g/2oz mozzarella, grated
30ml/2 tbsp freshly grated Parmesan
shredded basil leaves, to garnish

1 Preheat the oven to 220°C/425°F/ Gas 7. Tear the basil leaves into small pieces. Add half to the scone mix before mixing to a soft dough. Set aside the remainder.

2 Knead the dough gently on a lightly floured surface until smooth. Roll out and use to line a 30 x 18cm/12 x 7in Swiss-roll tin. Push up the edges to make a thin rim.

3 Brush the base with 15ml/1 tbsp of the tomato oil, then spread over the tomato sauce. Scatter over the sun-dried tomatoes, olives and remaining basil.

4 Sprinkle the mozzarella and Parmesan over the pizza. Drizzle over the remaining tomato oil. Bake for about 20 minutes. Cut lengthways and across into 24 bite-size pieces. Garnish with extra shredded basil leaves and serve immediately.

Farmhouse Pizza

This is the ultimate party pizza. Packed with tasty ingredients, it has a robust flavour that hungry guests will love. Served cut into fingers, it is ideal for a crowd.

Serves 8

90ml/6 tbsp olive oil
225g/8oz button mushrooms, sliced
2 quantities Basic (*see* page 16) or
     Superquick Pizza Dough (*see* page 18)
1 quantity Tomato Sauce (*see* page 21)
300g/10oz mozzarella, thinly sliced
115g/4oz wafer-thin smoked ham slices
6 bottled artichoke hearts in oil, drained
     and sliced
50g/2oz can anchovy fillets, drained and
     halved lengthways
10 pitted black olives, halved
30ml/2 tbsp chopped fresh oregano
45ml/3 tbsp freshly grated Parmesan
black pepper

1 Preheat the oven to 220°C/425°F/ Gas 7. Heat 30ml/2 tbsp of the oil in a large frying pan, add the mushrooms and fry for about 5 minutes until all the juices have evaporated. Leave to cool.

2 Roll out the dough on a lightly floured surface to a 30 x 25 cm/12 x 10in rectangle. Transfer to a greased baking sheet then push up the dough edges to make a thin rim. Brush with 30ml/2 tbsp of the oil.

3 Spread over the tomato sauce.

4 Arrange the sliced mozzarella so that it is slightly overlapping on top of the sauce.

5 Scrunch up the ham and arrange over the cheese, then add the artichoke hearts, mushrooms and anchovies.

6 Dot with the olives, then sprinkle over the oregano and Parmesan. Drizzle over the remaining oil and season with black pepper. Bake for about 25 minutes until crisp and golden. Serve immediately.

COOK'S TIP
This pizza can be quickly made with some storecupboard ingredients such as canned olives and anchovies and bottled artichoke hearts, then topped with whatever cheese you have to hand.

Feta, Pimiento and Pine Nut

Delight your guests with these tempting pizzas. Substitute goat's cheese for the feta if you prefer. Pine nuts add a crunchy contrast to the cheese.

2 Spread a thin layer of the black olive tapenade on each oval and crumble over the feta.

3 Cut the pimiento into thin strips and pile on top.

4 Sprinkle each one with thyme and pine nuts. Drizzle over the remaining oil and grind over plenty of black pepper. Bake for 10–15 minutes until crisp and golden. Garnish with thyme sprigs and serve immediately.

Makes 24

2 quantities Basic (*see* page 16) or
    Superquick Pizza Dough (*see* page 18)
60ml/4 tbsp olive oil
30ml/2 tbsp black olive tapenade
175g/6oz feta
1 large canned pimiento, drained
30ml/2 tbsp chopped fresh thyme
30ml/2 tbsp pine nuts
black pepper
thyme sprigs, to garnish

COOK'S TIP
Instead of canned pimiento, add some finely sliced red (bell) pepper.

1 Preheat the oven to 220°C/425°F/Gas 7. Divide the dough into 24 and roll out each piece on a floured surface to a small oval, about 3mm/⅛in thick. Prick all over with a fork. Brush with 30ml/2 tbsp of oil.

Mozzarella, Anchovy and Pesto

These unusual pizzas combine the piquancy of olives and capers with anchovies and mozzarella. Because they are so small, they make great canapés or party appetizers.

Makes 24

2 ready-to-cook pizza bases, about
    20cm/8in diameter
60ml/4 tbsp olive oil
30ml/2 tbsp red pesto
12 pitted black olives
75g/3oz mozzarella, cubed
50g/2oz (drained weight) sun-dried
    tomatoes in oil, chopped
30–45ml/2–3 tbsp capers
50g/2oz can anchovy fillets, drained and
    roughly chopped
30ml/2 tbsp freshly grated Parmesan
parsley sprigs, to garnish

3 Cut the olives into quarters lengthways, then scatter over the bases with the mozzarella, sun-dried tomatoes, capers and anchovies.

4 Sprinkle over the Parmesan and drizzle over the remaining oil. Bake for 8–10 minutes until crisp and golden. Garnish with parsley sprigs and serve immediately.

1 Preheat the oven to 220°C/425°F/Gas 7. Using a 5cm/2in plain round cutter stamp out 24 rounds from the pizza bases. Place the rounds on two greased baking sheets.

2 Brush the bases with 30ml/2 tbsp of the oil, then spread over the pesto.

Sun-dried Tomato Bread

This savoury bread tastes delicious on its own, but it also makes exceptional sandwiches.
For example, try a tasty filling of sliced tomatoes, basil leaves and grated Parmesan cheese.

Makes 1 loaf

375g/13oz/3¼ cups strong white (stone-
   ground) flour
5ml/1tsp salt
10ml/2tsp easy-blend dried yeast
50g/2oz (drained weight) sun-dried
   tomatoes in oil, chopped
175ml/6fl oz/¾ cup lukewarm water
75ml/5 tbsp olive oil, plus extra to brush
plain (all-purpose) flour for dusting

1 Sift the flour and salt into a large
mixing bowl.

2 Stir in the yeast and sun-dried
tomatoes.

3 Make a well in the centre of the dry
ingredients. Pour in the water and oil, and
mix until the ingredients come together
and form a soft dough.

4 Turn the dough on to a lightly floured
surface and knead for about 10 minutes.

COOK'S TIP
To freeze the bread so that it still tastes
fresh when it is thawed, wrap the bread in
foil or put in a sealed freezer bag to
exclude all the air. Always freeze the
bread the day that you make it. Once it
has defrosted, wrap it in foil and warm
through in a low oven.

5 Shape into an oblong loaf, without
making the top too smooth, and place on
a greased baking sheet. Brush the top
with oil, cover with clear film, then leave
to rise in a warm place for about 1 hour.

6 Meanwhile, preheat the oven to
220°C/425°F/Gas 7. Remove the clear
film, then sprinkle the top of the loaf
lightly with flour. Bake for 30–40 minutes
until the loaf sounds hollow when tapped
on the bottom. Serve warm.

Rosemary and Sea Salt Focaccia

Focaccia is an Italian flat bread made with olive oil. In this recipe, rosemary adds flavour and coarse sea salt provides a tasty crunch.

Makes 1 loaf

350g/l2oz/3 cups plain (all-purpose) flour
2.5ml/½ tsp salt
10ml/2tsp easy-blend dried yeast
about 250ml/8fl oz/1 cup
    lukewarm water
45ml/3 tbsp olive oil
1 small red onion
leaves from 1 large rosemary sprig
5ml/1tsp coarse sea salt

1 Sift the flour and salt into a large mixing bowl. Stir in the yeast, then make a well in the centre of the dry ingredients. Pour in the water and 30ml/2 tbsp of the oil. Mix well, adding a little more water if the mixture seems dry.

2 Turn the dough on to a lightly floured surface and knead for about 10 minutes until smooth and elastic.

VARIATION
Add sliced mushrooms, small cubes of pancetta, sliced olives or finely sliced red or yellow (bell) peppers.

3 Place the dough in a greased bowl, cover and leave in a warm place for about 1 hour until doubled in size. Knock back and knead the dough for 2–3 minutes.

4 Meanwhile, preheat the oven to 220°C/425°F/Gas 7. Roll out the dough to a large circle, about 1cm/½ in thick, and transfer to a greased baking sheet. Brush with the remaining oil.

5 Halve the onion and slice into thin wedges. Sprinkle over the dough, with the rosemary and sea salt, pressing in lightly.

6 Using a finger make deep indentations in the dough. Cover the surface with greased clear film, then leave to rise in a warm place for 30 minutes. Remove the clear film and bake for 25–30 minutes until golden. Serve warm.

Mini Focaccia with Pine Nuts

Pine nuts add little bites of nutty texture to these simple mini focaccias. They can be eaten cut into cubes and dipped into some extra virgin olive oil.

Makes 4 mini loaves

350g/12oz/3 cups plain (all-purpose) flour
2.5ml/½ tsp salt
10ml/2tsp easy-blend dried yeast
about 250ml/8fl oz/l cup lukewarm water
45ml/3 tbsp olive oil
45–60ml/3–4 tbsp pine nuts
10ml/2tsp coarse sea salt

1 Sift the flour and salt into a mixing bowl. Stir in the yeast, then make a well and pour in the water and 30ml/2 tbsp of the oil. Mix and add more water if the mixture is dry. Turn on to a floured surface and knead for 10 minutes until smooth and elastic.

2 Place the dough in a greased bowl, cover and leave in a warm place for about 1 hour until doubled in size. Knock back and knead the dough for 2–3 minutes.

3 Divide the dough into four pieces.

4 Using your hands pat out each piece on greased baking sheets to a 10 x 7.5cm/4 x 3in oblong, which is rounded at the ends.

5 Scatter over the pine nuts and press them into the surface. Sprinkle with salt and brush with the remaining oil. Cover with greased clear film and leave to rise for about 30 minutes.

6 Meanwhile, preheat the oven to 220°C/425°F/Gas 7. Remove the clear film and bake the focaccias for 15–20 minutes until golden. Serve warm.

Walnut Bread

The nutty flavour of this wonderfully textured bread is excellent. Try it toasted and topped with melting goat's cheese for a mouth-watering snack.

Makes 2 loaves

600g/1lb 5oz/4 cups strong white flour (stone-ground flour)
10ml/2tsp salt
10ml/2tsp easy-blend dried yeast
150g/5oz/1¼ cups chopped walnuts
60 ml/4 tbsp chopped fresh parsley
400ml/14fl oz/1⅔ cups lukewarm water
60ml/4 tbsp olive oil

1 Sift the flour and salt into a bowl. Stir in the yeast, walnuts and parsley.

2 Add the water and oil and mix to a soft dough. Turn on to a floured surface and knead for 10 minutes until smooth and elastic. Place in a greased bowl, cover and leave in a warm place for an 1 hour.

3 The dough should be doubled in size. Knock back and knead the dough for 2–3 minutes. Divide in half and shape each piece into a thick roll about 18–20cm/ 7–8in long. Place on greased baking sheets, cover with clear film and leave to rise for about 30 minutes.

4 Meanwhile, preheat the oven to 220°C/425°F/Gas 7. Remove the clear film, then lightly slash the top of each loaf. Bake for 10 minutes, then reduce the oven temperature to 180°C/3SO°F/Gas 4 and bake for 25-30 minutes until the loaves sound hollow when tapped.

Olive Bread

Green olives are added to heighten the flavour of this moist bread. Use a combination of green and black olives if you prefer, or those stuffed with pimiento.

Makes 2 loaves

700g/llb 8½oz/6 cups strong white flour
    (stone-ground flour)
5ml/1tsp salt
sachet of easy-blend dried yeast
15ml/1 tbsp chopped fresh oregano
350ml/12fl oz/1½ cups lukewarm water
105ml/7 tbsp olive oil
about 30 pitted green olives

1 Sift the flour and salt into a large mixing bowl. Stir in the yeast and oregano.

2 Mix the water and 90 ml/6 tbsp of the oil. Make a well in the dry ingredients, pour in the liquid and mix to a soft dough.

3 Turn the dough on to a lightly floured surface and knead for about 10 minutes until smooth and elastic. Place in a greased bowl, cover with clear film and leave in a warm place for about 1 hour until doubled in size.

4 Knock back and knead the dough for 2–3 minutes. Divide in half, then press the dough on greased baking sheets into two ovals, about 1cm/½in thick.

COOK'S TIP
If you want to freeze Olive Bread, wrap in foil or put in a freezer bag, exclude air and seal. Freeze for up to 1 month.

5 Using your clean finger to make about 15 deep indentations over the surface of each loaf. Press an olive into each indentation.

6 Brush the loaves with the remaining oil, cover with clear film and leave to rise for about 30 minutes. Meanwhile, preheat the oven to 220°C/425°F/Gas 7. Remove the clear film and bake for 20–25 minutes until the loaves sound hollow when tapped. Serve the bread warm.

Saffron and Basil Breadsticks

Saffron lends its delicate aroma and flavour, as well as rich yellow colour, to these tasty breadsticks. Serve with a tomato, mozzarella and basil salad for a light meal.

Makes 32

generous pinch saffron strands
450g/1lb/4 cups strong white flour
    (stone-ground flour)
5ml/1 tsp salt
10ml/2tsp easy-blend dried yeast
300ml/½ pint/1¼ cups lukewarm water
45ml/3 tbsp olive oil
45ml/3 tbsp chopped fresh basil

1 Infuse the saffron strands in 30ml/ 2 tbsp hot water for 10 minutes.

2 Sift the flour and salt into a bowl. Stir in the yeast, then make a well in the centre of the dry ingredients. Pour in the water and saffron liquid and start to mix a little.

3 Add the oil and basil and continue to mix to a soft dough.

4 Turn out and knead the dough on a lightly floured surface for about 10 minutes until smooth and elastic. Place in a greased bowl, cover with clear film and leave for about 1 hour until it has doubled in size.

COOK'S TIP
Saffron comes from the dried stigmas of the saffron crocus, and is picked by hand, hence its high price. Saffron comes in strands and powder, and both should be a bright orange-red colour, never yellow.

5 Knock back the dough then turn on to a lightly floured surface and knead for 2–3 minutes.

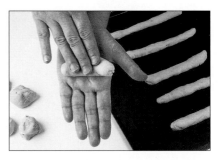

6 Preheat the oven to 220°C/425°F/Gas 7. Divide the dough into 32 pieces and shape into long sticks. Place well apart on greased baking sheets, then leave for a further 15–30 minutes until they become puffy. Bake for about 15 minutes until crisp and golden. Serve warm.

Index